Creamsicle Stick Shivs

Books by John Stiles

Poetry
Scouts Are Cancelled (2002)

Novel
The Insolent Boy (2001)

Creamsicle Stick Shivs

poems by John Stiles

A 4 A.M. BOOK

INSOMNIAC PRESS

Library and Archives Canada Cataloguing in Publication

Stiles, John, 1966-
    Creamsicle stick shivs / John Stiles.

Poems.
ISBN 1-897178-18-2

    I. Title.

PS8587.T554C74 2006   C811'.6   C2005-907615-1

The publisher gratefully acknowledges the support of the Canada Council, the Ontario Arts Council and the Department of Canadian Heritage through the Book Publishing Industry Development Program.

Printed and bound in Canada

Insomniac Press
192 Spadina Avenue, Suite 403
Toronto, Ontario, Canada, M5T 2C2
www.insomniacpress.com

This book is dedicated to my landlady in Toronto.

Contents

Part 1
Halifax Snowstorm

Halifax Snowstorm	11
House for the Rural Poor	12
Seeyoor Boy	13
New Pile for Road	14
Gourds, Melons, Waterville Incarcerations	15
Class A Stink	16
Felt Like Cryin	17
Sumpin Foolish, Anyhow	18

Part 2
Creamsicle Stick Shivs

Fouled on Pitch	21
Page 67, Ripped	22
Bus Ride with Ecuadorian Fellow	23
Painful Exercises in Self-Implosion	24
Mr. Dinkmouth	25
Les Sondage	26
Creamsicle Stick Shivs	27
Pills, Decongestants I Believe	28
A Moron Is About 60 or So	29
These Men Are Not Pimps, After All!	30
Not the One for You, Hilly	31
Your Man in the Kitchen	32
Whisper My Blue Eyes	33
Poplars	34
Two Short Ones	36
Distance, Please, Sir	37
Interlude	38

Part 3
Meritimer in London

Happy Till Your Wife Gets a Job in a Bar   41
Landlady at the Top of the Staircase   42
Oh, About the Money   43
Rice from the Iceland   44
New American Writing (at Dinnertime)   45
Trip Out to Brighton   47
The Comedy Club Was Closed   48
Shitty Ditty: Meritimer in London   49
Creep at the Church Charity   50
Nice Boy in a Church Pew   51
Gaylord in Delhi   52
Sorry State of the Conqueror   53
Women, When They Get Fed Up   54
Last Day Before the 24th   56
Meritimer in London   58
Moment in the Carol Service   59
Birthday Party for a Ninety-Year-Old   60
Can't Get My Head around Canada   61
Little Incident Down the Lincoln's Inn   62

Afterword   65
Acknowledgements   69
Notes   71

I

Halifax Snowstorm

Halifax Snowstorm

I ask you this: I gotta chase you halfway across
the goddamned world? Yell yer name in alleyways,
lay down my sleeping bag like the world is one
big mud puddle, hold yer little hand en pull my rowing
jacket over that mess a blue black hair, whilst all you do
is pout en whisper that yer gynaecologist is cuter than I am?

Well it's true: I do stand like a soldier in the parking lot
with yer grocery bags. But Jesus girl, wouldja take off
yer goddamned top en let that stunnin church of a tit
fall out your blouse, so we can turn our heads en waltz
like two goddamned lovestruck swans cross the rooftop
in this glorious Halifax Snowstorm?

House for the Rural Poor
(for the Greenfield Mountain folk)

I do not come in the door with shame, Moira.
I come through that screen door to fix it.
So I got a bottle a Moody Blue en a violin,
I'll set with the kids en my brother,
en there'll be no smokin cause I know it bothers you.

We'll play familiar songs tell I start to nod off
en I go oat the cab en I lay in back the truck
with the dog en I know that you got the stove on still.

Where me en the ol feller live now, we get water
from a brook, back in the day I used to snare rabbits
when I wasn't skippin school.

I never took a wife for personal reasons
but I do think of you in that way, Moira,
en I know that my brother don't know me
like you seen me after pickin season.

It's the nights that get lonely en cold that's why
I come round these parts as I'm known to do.
There's certain ways a man has, en tonight I can tell
you know why I look the way I do.

Seeyoor Boy

Near beat Bluebell en Mildred in back of Varney's barn.
Yoke near broke en the cats was millin round.

Twine hung like a gallows, notches dug in staves.
Cruel smile from the wife, Bernadette, half cut? Doubt that boy.

Last time she hit the bottle I fell off a crate
down Bills Lunch with the stepson.

New Pile for Road

Down the dykes the Caterpillar and Mac truck
are in union: sand and muck slung down
a wave from a bored man in cab to a quarry.
   Dig. Dug. Done.

Down we go, to the pathway, Dad and I, this all
will go, this all denied, the simple, the slow,
the silence you hear in your bed at night:
   a pheasant runs.

Can it be that the farm takes bus tours?
This was your home. The neighbours
you hid from in the fruit trees: the scout leader,
   his son, the doll player.

He's there in the ol chipped house,
was stuck in a learning carrel in grade six.
Never got over it, though he was lazy
most his life, hated to turn the earth.

And he has no feelings at all for the ol Mac truck.

Gourds, Melons, Waterville Incarcerations
(for Lars)

Peter had an ol gourd size of a softball,
gumboots up round his knees. He was like a pirate
up back, goin sumars, I do not know!
Knife short of a picnic? *Did not know he could hold one!*
Shears, I think they was, rusted right out.

Young mun, spun his head to the side, sung.
Flowing white shirt, razor burn, legs like sticks, sumpin.
Somun sayeed: He's like a cat, steppin over the peas.
Cute, fer a feller in jeans.

Shears? Friggen rights! They was left in the dump,
blades like a propeller! Will you stab the earth
with that trowel? Not much higher than a grapevine
might grow, trap flies, if the blessed sun ever did shine.

Class A Stink

Em broilers made some Class A stink
whin a muskrat shimmied unner the conveyor:
Ratty Ratty Ratty in the hole, boy.
Holy Cow! Holy Mo!

Rottin iggs? I'm not *seyooor* boy.
See em cowflies buzz en saw?
Rotten iggs? Pong. Pong. Pongy Ponger
Pong Ping Pongo: *Isn't that sumpin?*

I'll tell youse now that light come in slants.
Em chickens set like peasants who sacked
the court a the king.

Felt Like Cryin

Mr. Simpson went oat Bills Lunch like a house on fire
with his pack a Craven A up his arm like a box.

Em fers at the counter was watchin him like hawks en
whin one of em asked if I'd like a pack a O-Pee-Chee,
I told em I'd take a dollars wortha bologna instead.

En whin I set there gnawin on the thing like Shep done
her bone, I saw a big bulldozer pass en Fulton got
talking boat the pile a money Mr. Simpson made whin
    he sold off the Orchard.

En whin I thought about Shep pissing on Mr. Simpson's
flower bed, I felt like cryin, when I thoughta Shep, glassy
eyes in Mr. Simpson's headlights, all set to go the way
    ol Major gone.

Sumpin Foolish, Anyhow
(For Darren Greer)

> *Chummy. Lummy. Fulla. Wanna.*
> *Hanger? Dingy? Danga! Donger!!*

Picturing: good-natured VON nurse, doing house calls,
clipping toenails, running bathwater to soften corns and bunions.

Overhearing: sumpin you seen last night hangin socks
on the line, could see right through her skirt, the outline
of her legs. The fuller, none too bright, on the tricycle's goin,

> *How's she hangin, fuller?*

Mom's goin git inside the house en set on the toilet
tell I come inside. The goof with the grin on the tricycle's goin,

> *Uhhhhuhuuhuhhhhhh.*

Cat is the smart one, tail like a question mark, he's around
yer mothers legs like a mink shawl. Erin's on the toilet, you know
cause you can hear the bowl flushin the bathroom above.

En the screen door is flappin open like the mouth
on the stunned fuller on the tricycle going round en round
like sumpin right foolish, anyhow.

2
Creamsicle Stick Shivs

Fouled on Pitch

A tall, lanky man in sneakers, shirt out the back
like a sail, fly down, mulling a remark from a sceptical
teacher: *Are you selling cigars, Monsieur?*

Oh God. Pardon me. You look down. Some girl
standing on the pitch like a tree. You say
pass the ball, and they say, *It's all in fun, Monsieur.*

You try to keep up. Can you imagine? Give the ball
a kick, bend it round the two frenchies
who pass like two determined boys at ping pong.

You take the ball hard, collapse, *My God!*
They ask, *Are you alright, Sir?* and you say,
*I've hurt myself. Please excuse me if I forget to do
    roll call in the morning.*

Page 67, Ripped

Quite honestly I stole this line from a student,
the troubled one who had a laser stare when girls spoke.

One day he had a tape recorder. He was tape recording
everything that went on with his friend Adrien, just the
    everyday details.

I think he thought it was absurd. Students in grade eleven
making bristol board posters, talking about being good

Catholiques when kids were rioting in the halls. He mentioned
something about teachers legging it out of the school at the end
    of day.

I wanted to tell him about the terror of SARS,
the panic that I feel at times, but I don't want him to worry,
he deserves the best, an original thinker,

one of the lucky chickens that made it out of the battery
that is the Dufferin Peel School System.

Bus Ride with Ecuadorian Fellow

Sitting hunched in the bus, driving
towards the French penal colony
with an Ecuadorian fellow,
Ram rod tight, he's ready to pop
off the seat. He calls you *The Professor,*
chats up all the girls, flipping through
your Cole's Notes – Hamlet?

Cole's Notes you give him: *Where
is the soliloquy, Professor?
Do you like young men, Professor?
If you were a young man
would you have a one in a million
chance with me, Professor?*

*You are Italian the way that you move
your hands,* says the other one,
the Argentinean whose parents
keep an eye on him. *I can't even go
to Canada's Wonderland,* he says,
they'll start calling me on my cell phone.

Painful Exercises in Self-Implosion

This, while racked in pain, pulling leg by leg from the
    bed at 10 a.m.
This, while realizing the trip to the library will be in the
    same clothing as the day before, most likely the week
    before.
This, while reading through a first novel, first draft, in
    astonishment at the sound structure, suicidal at the prose.
This, while pulling grey hairs from your nose.
This, while eating a tin of creamed rice, feeling a tooth chipped.
This, while putting off tidying, vacuuming, writing that Tobias
    Smollett review: trying to explain a fiery red-headed Scot only
    you can love.

Mr. Dinkmouth

Mr. Dinkmouth goes wandering down the alleyway
    with his bag of books, scurrying, looking over his shoulder.
He was a sensitive child, I suppose, though I wouldn't have
    shown him no mercy. Jesus what a stoop he has at fifty-five.
Stand up, Mr. Dinkmouth. Mr. Dinkmouth, gimme your money
    at recess and that box of your raisins in your palm.
Mr. Dinkmouth with his cats at night in his bed-sit, heating
    pad, remembers the shadows in the tent at church camp
    with the bully who stood like a shadow, threw slate stone
    through the roof, the armies of ants in his nose.
Get up, Mr. Dinkmouth!
The rage of Mr. Dinkmouth. The pain of Mr. Dinkmouth.
Stand up, Mr. Dinkmouth. Be a man, Mr. Dinkmouth.
Don't try be so kind to the ladies, Mr. Dinkmouth,
    they don't pity you or dress you up nice for the assembly
    again.

Les Sondage

Monsieur in a white coat, front of the class,
about to write on the board, about poetry.
Tone. Tempo. Rhythm. Narration. Lyric. Some
young fluffy chap, grade twelve, comes in, goes on
about *Les Sondage.* Oh Christ, why not?

You lean back, heads behind hands,
kick up, *en français,* it is all *en français*
and you would do the same down the valley,
mimic the idiot who took over band class.

Creamsicle Stick Shivs

I think I might have to knock you out.
I think I may have to stab you
in the eye with my fork, really.

You are on some kind of bad trip.
Some days I lose it just thinking
about how I might fall to pieces
staring into my plate. Watch out!!!

I'll take the Creamsicle sticks
from the craft show, fashion
them into shivs. I just might
stand like a stuffed onion, yell
horrid things to the old ladies
poring over their home baking,
all those delicious tarts and pies.

Pills, Decongestants I Believe

My mom, who is on pills, and my sister, also on pills,
are all smiley till the phone rings and it's my sister's lawyer.

My dad, who is a breadwinner and sad of late, is now
at a CFL game in Hamilton cheering the boatmen.

That cunning bastard – like there is something wrong
with being happy, something wrong with being that tall
man with sideburns in the airport, clenching his hands

in the air. This gentleman and this lawyer affair nearly
broke his heart – I believe all that money spent on a
    wedding.

He'll get through it, but it's me that has the cold and is
    drugged out

on these pills, these decongestants, I believe, so I'll email
this dark-haired beauty I'm mad for and wait like a child
    for her to email me in the morning.

A Moron Is About 60 or So

I took an online IQ test today
and this test said I have an IQ
of 132. So does this mean
that I am fairly stupid, when
I went to school with a bunch
of clever clogs who claimed
they were in the 170–200 range?

*(This was online, during the day,
with the boss looking over
my shoulder as she punched
numbers into her adding machine.)*

If most are in the 100 range,
then a moron is about 60 or so,
and I am slightly above average.
I feel like a little kid hoisted
onto his fathers shoulders,
realising: *no more sweets for you.*

These Men Are Not Pimps, After All!

Still I get on and off the bus at random,
try to walk to work, to keep the weight down
and hoard candy bar wrappers in my coat.

I write phrases of books I'll never write,
phrases like: *seasoned delight*.
I try to explain how the morons
on the London Night Bus were talking
about women as though they were hitting on elderly ladies.

This, after pulling some scrap from my pants:
Relax, these men were not pimps, after all!

Not the One for You, Hilly

Do you have any way of telling me
that you don't love me anymore
other than apologizing to your gay
friend because I slept in his bed?

When you don't love me anymore,
am I like the one who called me
from the airport in tears, saying
but I don't love her – how could I?

I love you, you silly girl, the cassettes
you sent me with the photo of us
on Lawrencetown beach, this
soppy shit I hide from friends.

How you set me up for love, how we were
in my hometown with the cats.
You left me in the bath, called me Nippy,
then drove home to your mother.

Perhaps I should write this for her –
did she have words with you after
dinner, did she politely remind you
that I was not the one for you?

Your Man in the Kitchen

So kindly and confidentially I caress you. So
carefully and quietly I fall down from the tree
to greet you, hold you as you make your grand

entrance in gumboots and woollen skirt. We are
together, and so we go through the hallways, sister,
mother in a white gown twisting hands through

the air like an old lady singing along to a radio song.
Scooting round the Maple Tree, with skirts up, gasping
at the jokes, rude enough, but clever enough

to make you fancy the fish salesman on the porch
and forget about me, your temporary project, your
contemporary dishwasher, piler of plates, your man

in the kitchen: have I lost face now that you have
caught me counting stitches in the rocking chair?

Whisper My Blue Eyes

I'm forcing myself to trust again
and enjoying trusting people.

I'm giving myself a regular
examination, not taking things too literal.

I've gone through the fuzz
in the pockets, tweezed the ingrown hairs,

sucked the green puss
from an ingrown toenail.

I've gone through the peanut trays.
Pretzels anyone?

I wait in expectation on the couch
for you to arrive. Just for you.

And just because I wait for you,
will I admit I want you to bite my nose?

Smile, my dear, and whisper
my blue eyes in the morning.

Poplars

Even when I was young I was caught staring at the girls.
I used to show off on the teeder-todder in the schoolyard
near the wood of poplars. Love hearts etched into the
black ridges of smoke, skinny trees that crowned the

soccer pitch like wild hair. Who would have thought the
awkward boy reading *Teahouse of the August Moon*
would be the one college girls wrote notes to, pinned
on napkins in the Acadia cafeteria.

A sullen teen in tight velour pants, shadowed by the
rough boys who lined the walls of the gymnasium like
convicts. I remember my darling girlfriend, clenched
like a starfish on the back of some idiot, punching me
    in the face.

On George's Island I stared at the camp flames. Hil
told me the female praying mantis bites the head off
the male after they have intercourse. I told her I nearly
drowned in Waterton Park. Okayama-ken. Frogs croaking

in the tanbo, me brushing my teeth, the expression on
Lance's face when I told the Eki twins to go home. They waited
under the porch with drinks. Lance paced across the
veranda. Out the window twin girls bicycled, skirts fluttering.

In Nova Scotia my boss pressed her keys into my palm.
I knew it was all wrong when I saw her bodysurfing at her

cottage with my mother. My first year at college I loved a
valley girl three times, watched the moonlight like diamonds

on her shoulders as she walked naked through my room.
When I saw her look a sight in an artsy hat, I whispered,
something wicked this way comes, then quietly disappeared
into the column shadows of the Arts and Admin building.

I really had no idea, at the age of thirty-one, that you would
leave me walking down College Street with eight beers in me,
wishing I was on my way to you, cause in my mind its me
and you tangled in that smoke-black hair, that cluster of
poplars down them grassy fields where I come from.

Two Short Ones

I
The Vile Accoutrement

Okay so moustache, bad stache,
dead caterpillar on upper lip.
Can you see this repeated to
a fifth grade bud who drove
a skidoo over a cornfield
en left her there to rot?

II
Are You Feeling Hysterical?

Or is this just the way you read publicly?

Distance, Please, Sir

One desperate poet taking a column
to review the selected work of some drip
who flips papers on the floor and attacks
websites has seen me come in and the waiter

asks me if I'd like to take the backroom or sit
at the bar and I realize the initial impression
is not a good one and so I ask if the toilets
are located in the back or downstairs and I say

I was looking for my friend but the waiter
doesn't buy it exactly and so I'm sitting
on the toilet in the basement wondering
if I can remember his name as I run

the water in the sink and count my blessings
that I never had nor ever will own a cell phone.

Interlude

True story: I was flogging the *Globe and Mail* in a crummy office block in Toronto a few years back when I started jawing away to this ol Italian gent living in Victoria, B.C. He said: "Okay. Okay. Listen up, you mange cake. I can see you got the gift of the gab. And I appreciate a good newspaper, even if it costs two, three bones. Now you won't find a better listener in this household but I swear on my dead grandmother I won't be buying any of what you are selling."

This took me by surprise because we were having quite the chin wag, so I said: "Well, you know, sir, I'm still single and my mum told me behind every successful man is a good woman. Maybe I'm sounding too desperate."

"Desperate! Listen, you big idiot. You can never lose that, never, never, never! Every time I come in the house, my wife, she smile at me. And I've been happily married for fifty years, three kids and eight grandkids. But just so you know: *Women only really love you twice in life! Before you are married and after you are dead!*"

3
Mertimer in London

Happy Till Your Wife Gets a Job in a Bar

Are you the type to race down the street after your wedding ring?
Go back and forth between bar and office, pace Blackfriars
Bridge? The security guard calling you: *Don't you want in?*

Panicking about the wedding ring beside your bedside table,
when you get home. Why is it you always lose your keys,
get hit in the head with a newspaper by the old Irish guy?

Your wife smells like a bar. It's like sleeping with an ashtray,
still you wait for her. Probably she will be drinking,
and she is telling you that she will die the way things are going,

she will die the way that you don't want her to have any friends.
It was happiness together and she would rather walk to work
in the rain and sleep on the couch. She has the place

the way you want it, but will it ever be the way that she
      wants it?
You are happily married till your wife gets a job in a bar.

Landlady at the Top of the Staircase

Landlady at the top of the stairs sayin,
I have overlooked more than three-hundred
pounds for which you will not be charged.

Girlfriend on the bed sayin, *Irina, is it personal?*
Irina with her great fur hat, a Cossack, an old spinster,
mouth turned down – her poor husband.

I'll be away. I need you to make this decision
today or tomorrow.
Tears on the bed for two days.

Still, the landlady says, *John,*
I feel for your girlfriend.
She reminds me of my mother – back in the old days.

Oh, About the Money

About the money, things are tense,
so the dishes are done very slowly,
so beautiful and savage in a vest.

My dark-haired wife, tears in the sink,
someone is waiting to crack,
which one might that be?

I can tell you I feel like I'm sandwiched
between a miserable person
and a happy-go-lucky layabout.

What is the relationship between
people who don't do much, just
do some stuff, what stuff is that?

The stuff we do. I'd rather
just write, and she doesn't
say much, but just the other day

my wife was telling me how
good-looking I am. *Many girls
would go for you,* she said.

You are sharming. My wife
looks into the ceiling.
You are sharming, she says.

Rice from the Iceland

Last week we didn't have hardly any
money and we need to be in agreement.
We are on a very strict budget,
but can you go to the store to get some rice?
I don't like the rice from the other store –
I like the rice from the Iceland.

I thought you would buy some cheese
but you didn't – I like cheddar, so I'm
going to sit here on the couch and wait
for you. Don't worry, I will be
thinking about you while I read my book.

New American Writing (at Dinnertime)

We're both high strung about the state of the apartment,
me about getting some money into the bank account,
paying for our trips ahead of time. She is most always
    right:

it would be good to go to Halifax and leave from Toronto,
we could see everyone and not waste time or money,
we don't have much. My wife cooked today and did the
    dishes.

She doesn't sound impressed when I say I'll do the dishes,
but I would you see, I waited three years for her and I'm
still trying to impress her. If you ever had the chance to see
    my wife,

she would knock you out, she is so beautiful, big eyes,
and she bites my nose when she's in a good mood.
She did say congratulations on your publication.

My boss said some horrible thing to me today about
Canada. I can see she doesn't believe it. She is Miss Marple
in disguise, perhaps she is a writer with a mean view of men.

I Googled an old girlfriend today. She used to use words like
'glorious' in her travel writing. I wanted to say to my boss,
why don't you tell your kids that you love them, try not winding them
    up so much?

She did say that it was sport and that she was wicked sometimes. I wish I didn't have to work with so many women. It is a little tense. Sometimes I feel like we are all waiting for something, and so I say something foolish, which is not what they want at all.

Trip Out to Brighton

Trip out to Brighton on the Megabus, lights on coming back,
Indians crowded in front, love hearts traced on windows.
Me with wife holding hands, sister in front reading the
insert. I got this from the floor. It isn't dirty or interesting.

I should have got another pint. *Bah.* Wife trying to sleep
on my shoulder, this does not work; she is always putting
her head down somewhere, looking at peace with a big
smile. We will be back next week, and the next, *won't we?*

Every week someone says, *To Brighton?* Your parents
will love it. If there is a church, I say. This is the part
that is for sure, this is the part that my wife didn't know
before, nor did I wish to tell her from my little room in Toronto.

The Comedy Club Was Closed

Insanity: pinched into the front
of a Streatham Bus with a hooded
nutter fingering a Bible whilst the bus
stalls in Brixton. My love says look
there is a Register Office while some
sour labourer said into his mobile
that he was gonna *do someone in.*

Is this our society when we treat our
old people like lepers, our kids like ghouls
in restaurants begging at tables?
You are telling me that hair is for sale
whilst children are stabbed to death
and left to freeze in the snowy parks
of St. Peterbourgh. Who are our leaders
now? *Is a schoolmate running
for the Leadership of the NDP?**

*(N.B. P.C. Party, actually)

Shitty Ditty: Meritimer in London

Scuse me? You want some fluid for the photocopier?
Right on. I'll sort out the world later, bin the dust,
take my stuff off yer desk. Sorry about yer cough,
seems to be catching: *Cough. Retch. Choke.*

I had a bad night last night myself. Think I might
take a job as a bus driver to sort out the dire finances.
Wouldn't dream of doing that back in T dot O.
Is there something wrong with a guy who can't sit

still? Sorry, feeling a bit giddy. But I just wanted
to know – I don't claim to be the most intelligent
fellow goin – but now you've been waving the flag
of St. Kitts at me all afternoon, can I ask you one thing?

Are you a bottom-dwelling chummy with crummy bummy?

Creep at the Church Charity

I got a bad vibe from the guy who lent me
his letter opener. He looked at me
as if to say *hello, you are not supposed to be there.*

I don't think he had much in the way of emotion.
I thought: what if I struck up a conversation with him
and he plotted ways to dispose of my body

whilst he lent me his letter opener and then
came back to get it, what if he said *a short me
is not forever* and calmly slid the opener back

like he was putting a knife back into its sheath?

Nice Boy in a Church Pew

Nice boy in the pew of a church stamps cheques, invoices.
A faint-hearted little wren sails through the window, elated
in the sunlight, spied by a middle-aged cat. Claws as pricks
and bristles scraping the flesh: Get stuck in, you little midge!
The stapler is a weapon. You've sheets to stack and stamp!

Gaylord in Delhi

Manager in accounts at the church charity
emails the first floor to announce his wife
will treat the staff now that all the auditors
have packed up. Out comes the food, plates
of cheese sticks, veggies en dip: everyone
standing around an awkward circle,
the Bishop of Swindon in pants too tight.

Caroline from IT, not there, so the old Irish guy
called her a Hoover-on-legs. The wedding photos
are passed around. There're black ladies in hats
en the Bishop is there, talking about the Chinese
café, his trip to India. Frozen face when I say,
try the Gaylord in Delhi. These people really
know how to party. Everyone is so full.

They settle at their computers, after the drinks,
to tap away on the keys like crows over carrion.

Sorry State of the Conqueror

Sorry state of the conqueror wearing a helmet, the sad
eyes, shocks of blond hair, or is it grey? Demanding with a stake,
a trident that the little boats queue up to

– it's tax time, or was that last year? There was a time
when heart mattered, when they would say, *he is owed*.
But now the accountants are adjusting. They wear jeans
and slacks, polo shirts, make wise cracks

round a TV set. Hang them up by their toes, wring them
out or line them up in little boats, brain them all, beat them
all senseless. The mist is thick and the wind sounds like ghouls

in the morning after the auditor's been in. Call them blood-
hounds, assassins. Make no mistake – a matter of pennies
  will do you in.

Women, When They Get Fed Up

Typing feverishly while the auditors mill about,
wonder why the keys get stuck in the computer,
should I order a calculator cause I spilled coffee
all over the damned thing?

Laugh at Phil's jokes. He's waiting to call you
on his mobile perhaps, will you call him back?
Wife across the road going to the toilets likes
the decor of the restaurant,

but you say I don't like crowds or the cheeseburger.
She's not impressed you don't want to shop for music
for your father's birthday. But you do actually, Ella
or Frank, how to make a decision?

The Rat Pack will do, not knowing you can do better.
A call from a friend at 8 a.m. calling about stuff
he wants to do with you. He seems calm most of the time
till the manic bursts, the confessions.

He spends his time on 'oliday with his brother in Wales
and his parents are in their eighties. The screaming
from room to room, mother to son, and brother to father.
You don't want to know that part.

He confesses things to you about his personal life.
He seems hysterical in a quiet way. Just imagine
going out with him! At least with women, when
they get fed up, they leave.

Last Day Before the 24th

I hate Christmas. How many times have you
heard that from the old dear who sits at the back
with headphones on? Watch out. I might explode!
Teeth like a giant fence. I need to get married.

Why not? Will you pray for me? Introduce me
to Mr. Right? *A nice Canadian?* Where are you
off to this Christmas? You are handing out change,
twenty broken down: ten, five, five ones. No,

make that two fives, okay? Shall we share a meal,
a pint, at The Stage Door? It's a good pub.
When Jack gets back, we'll really tie one on.
If we can afford it. I'll send you a postcard

from the Caribbean. Mrs. Greengrass who writes
letters right up and around the page always addresses
the Financial Secretary. Isn't it romantic, even if
he might be a little...*you know?* I was attached

to the church charity in a missionary position.
This was fifty years ago. My sister was a soldier
of the Lord in the Diocese of Bonda, or was that
Southwest Tanganika? I was interested in hearing

the Bishop of Swindon. I hear he is very good.
Here is forty pounds. Please do not allocate this
to the General Fund. A *Gift Aid Form*
is enclosed. No receipt required. It is good to see

the money go to the deserving, not to pad the pockets
of the office clerks. I see Miss Helveg passed on. Shall we
send a collection round? How can it be possible to *Gift Aid*
someone who cannot and will no longer answer the phone?

Meritimer in London

A brutal hairdo and forms to fill out,
bootin er up Brixton Hill, gabbin bout
timesheets, housing, benefit forms, post office.

Thank you, Mr. Clerk. I know you just
want to get me off the phone, out the queue.
Yes you took the wrong turn, cause you
want to get it out of your system, sorry about that.

The buses are jammed and you are on
your way to Golders Green. You need
to sit down, stare out the window, remember
what it was that you had plans to do originally.

Moment in the Carol Service

The men asked private questions after
the Carol Service. They were picking
at chicken, filleting a mince tart
    with a thumb.

Are you embarrassed by the big-hearted gal
roaming round the table with a glass of wine
she is determined to give to the shy fellow
    who scoots along?

Would you have been singing as you did
if you did not feel that it was strange to have
the churchy folk in front of you looking
    like a city skyline:

one tall, the other short, two falling-down buildings
propping each other up? Then the one you thought
was a little shrew, like a budgie released from its cage,
she opens that nasty little beak and sings.

Birthday Party for a Ninety-Year-Old

A marquee in the garden, red wine, cold meat trays
and relatives who remember the blond boy from down the
    lane.

Isn't he elegant, says your ninety-year-old auntie,
and someone makes remarks about your trousers.

Your father's suit, you remind them. Simon does his
speech, after all, he's earned it, hasn't he?

Mum and Dad bring in the glassware and barely speak to
each other, though your Mum does say, *sometimes your
    father annoys me.*

It's all about the horses, the twelve acres in the back,
though your auntie has had her hair done in Witney,

oh yes, and wears a new dress. *Do you think
Judy looks frail?* asks your auntie.

I have to go and let out the dogs, says a cousin,
and off he goes like a rocket.

This, the women I devoted a book to, left in the dining room,
as I leave with my parents. She seems so sad, but I don't
think she is, actually. Never married, she is, wild white hair,
    pure as the driven snow.

Can't Get My Head around Canada

Must say I miss wandering up Harbord Street
in the stifling summer heat, drunk. Have you left
another message on the machine? *Hi John, it's Paul.*

How to explain this to my dear wife. She will cry when
my brother speaks after our wedding, says how I am a puzzle.
I think of you, Scouser, you've no friends here in Britain.

You go into bars trying to get to this Edinburgh Festival.
You talk for hours at a bus stop outside Trafalgar Square,
tell me, email me, that you have a gig, then talk shit

about my wife-to-be. *Who is on your arm now, a Brazilian?*
You are the best of a lousy bunch of poets in a place where
you have to pay to perform, the shit poet waving to the crowds.

Well, who cares now? You Scouser. You Scouser.
You took my book of poetry, said, *this stuff is alright
but I just can't get my head around Canada.*

Little Incident Down the Lincoln's Inn

The Ship, round the corner of Holborn,
was on the private tour up from the King
George IV, or the White Horse. Not far off,
the Lincoln's Inn Park. There is a memorial
there, to Canadians who fought in the First
World War. Quite the flourish of leaves.

Spencer Percival, shot at or near
the House of Commons, apparently
was the only British Prime Minister
assassinated. And Tony Blair, other
Prime Ministers, members of Lincoln's Inn.

Not Michael Howard, though. Not a Prime Minister!
Says the guide, well-spoken, mild halitosis,
and a flourish of the hand. *John Donne,* he says,
that dandy randy dandy, John Donne.

Afterword

How yah doon?

I moved to London, England last year. I was thirty-six. I came from the Annapolis Valley, via Toronto, having been sidetracked by a group of glum musicians, but I won't go into that now. (Smalls RIP. Corby, you are a lovely looking cowboy.) The reason I came was I had a revelation. I was lying in my bed on Shaw Street drunk one night, avoiding answering the phone, and I stared at the ceiling. I figured, amidst bursts of the desire to puke on the pile of bed clothing beside me, that if the Brits has exported their culture around the world, why couldn't we, Meritimers, export her right back?

Friggen Rights! Boys oh Boys!

So I packed my gumboots and long johns and laundry into a kit bag. Sent the computer surface mail cause I couldn't afford the fancy prices by air.

The first thing I noticed when I got to the U.K. was rows in the street. Couples in the U.K. could care less who's watching. They brace for the storm and have a go, matey. Kids in prams blink as couples implode. I've seen parents spank their kids in public, couple slap each other, mother and daughter hold out for a poolside barney. A gathering audience? No matter. This is Britain at its finest. These are the days of men with shaved heads holding the bikini strings of teenage birds puking on street corners.

It's like dis, yeah?

The difference between Brits and Canadians is manifold, but it's more than you'd think. I have a friend who's a comedian from Liverpool. I can't figure out a word he's saying. His comedy is built around his riding the night buses, trying to pick up women and complaining about his shoe fetish. A crazed stare, a smile and then, "Ooh. Ooh. Give us your shoe, luv!" He told me recently that he liked it when I did pet sounds when I was doing my Annapolis Valley poetry. So I stood on the corner, waiting for No. 159 to Streatham, and I gave him *Scouts Are Cancelled* to read. He told me he likes the siren and the dog groaning noises. He told me I was an odd character. He said, "I like your stories, man, but I can't get my head around Canada."

"Oh Canada? Or Canader," as my bud Bob from Plymouth used to say whilst firing cardboard boxes into a skip. "You guys are so laid back."

Canadians can have a conversation that isn't going anywhere. "Whatever...er whatever" and "Pipin' er" (Albertan). "Dummer than a sack full of hammers" and "tighter than a mouse's hole stretched over a barrel" (Nova Scotian). These are our expressions, and they're as idiosyncratic as the Brits who say "guv," "geezer" and use cockney slang. But Brits seem to need to prove a point, prove their mettle. Canadians seem aloof to all the intensity.

Recently I've started doing my poetry bit at the comedy clubs because the poets charge to perform here. Being popular in high school is no reason to decide you want to become a writer. Being an asshole is no reason to become a poet. But there you go.

Comedy/Poetry in London? Picture this, bud: Me, sipping on tepid rum 'n coke, slightly off-putting stare, and then...

How yah doon? My name is John. I'm calling from Bell Canada. The Globe and Mail, Canada's National Newspaper! We've invested in the Career, Arts and Sports sections. Why don't you flip to the front page? It's some nice lookin, now. No? Mrs. Farrell, you are tighter than a mouse's hole stretched over a barrel. Givver a whirl girl. No? Mr. Farrell? Why don't you givver a try, guy? Nope? I'm not asking you to finance my little man's education here. I'm not the tax man. Get your plastic out and pay for it with your pogey cheque. No skin off my arse.

I guess they empty out the jails and mental hospitals in the U.K., as well. Anybody here an impatient type? Can you imagine Woody Allen doing a house showing? Mixed groans from the Brits. Me saying, "Well, I know this here's the land of wit and rapport, eh, wha? You got your Oscar Wildes, your George Bernard Shaws and such like and so forth. Well we got a few down home. You got your Brainard and Maynard twins, and I seen a few Oscar Weirds in my day."

Oscar Weirds?

Next mission? Get them to say thank you. Polite but firm.

John Stiles

Acknowledgements

Some of the poems have appeared, often in earlier versions, in the following publications: *Lichen, The Literary Review of Canada, Taddle Creek Magazine, Polka Dot Ceiling* (U.K.), *nthposition* (U.K.), *Untitled* (U.K.), *Doom, Desire & Vice*, and *New American Writing* (U.S.).

The afterword originally appeared in *Broken Pencil* magazine as an essay entitled "Meritimer in London' and is used with their kind permission.

These poems are dedicated to the people I've met and who have helped me in my artistic path and/or who have inspired me in my path along the way: my wife, Veridiana, my parents, David and Wicky, my old friend, Corby "Judgement Day" Lund, Buddy, The Bishop of Swindon, Lars from Riga Drive in Wuffill, boy, Silas White, Mike Brooks at USPG, Paul Vermeersch, Sheila Heti, Ed Keenan, Mark Venturi, AJ Levin, Tobey Davies, Todd Swift, Andrew Copeman, Lee Wilson, Kevin Reinhart, Patrick Woodcock, Mike O'Connor and Christian C. Dunn. And who is on your arm now? A Brazilian?

Notes

This book was written in Toronto, Canada and London, England. The poems in this book have been performed in clubs and bars and cafés in Toronto and London, England.

The title of this book is derived from the idea that, despite our intentions, our natural inclination is not always to be a good boy, to do the right thing. No disrespect to church ladies or my parents, or my beloved maiden aunt and grandmother.

Contrary to public opinion, Canadians don't sound like Americans the more they live in London. However, they do tend to sound like Kermit the Frog.